Marvellous Mina

T0337781

Written by Joanna Nadin

Illustrated by Lesley Danson

Collins

Mina May Malek was born too early and got ill too often. All in all, she'd spent 14 months and 22 days in hospital. So her mum and dad worried about her a lot.

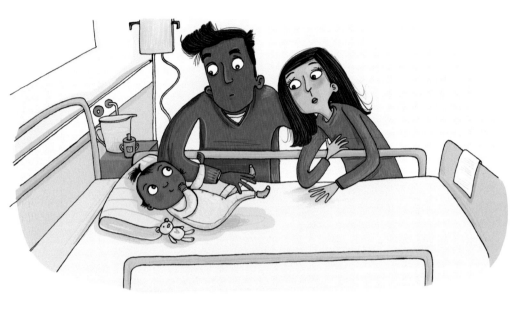

"Don't follow your brother up the tree, Mina!" cried Mum. "You might fall!"

"And don't put his roller skates on, Mina!" pleaded Dad. "You might crash!"

By the time she was nine, Mina May Malek hadn't been allowed to climb trees, roller skate, canoe, jump off a diving board, or even eat strawberries, while her big brother, Ayman, was allowed to do almost anything he liked.

Worst of all, she wasn't allowed to ride a stunt bike. Instead, she had to sit on the bench at the park reading a book. While Ayman bunny hopped …

and alley-ooped …

and barspinned …

and backflipped …

and rock walked.

More than anything in the world, Mina
May wanted to ride a bike like Ayman.

"Please?" she begged. "Please can I have
a go? I'll be ever so careful."

"Oh, I don't think so," worried Dad.

"Maybe next week," said Mum.

Mina May sighed. "You said that
last week. And the week before that.
And the week before that."

"You're just too small!" said Mum.

"You're just not strong enough!" said Dad.
"You need muscles to ride a bike."

Mina May sighed again. It was true
she was not much taller than a tall dog.
And there wasn't much she could do
about that.

But being strong? Well, there was
something she could change.

"I'll show them," she said to herself.
"I'll make myself as strong as an ox, and then
they can't say no."

And so she did.

Every morning before breakfast, Mina May Malek did
50 star jumps …

and 50 sit-ups …

and lifted as many books as she could in two
enormous bags.

At school, if anything heavy needed carrying, Mina May
offered to help out.

At playtime, she did pull-ups on the climbing frame.

At lunchtime, she joined in Ayman's football matches.

And after school, she zoomed round the playground as many times as she could before Dad came to pick them up.

For four whole weeks, she worked as hard as she could to be as strong as she could. Not quite as strong as an ox, but definitely as strong as Ayman.

"This is the week," she said to herself, as they walked to the park on Saturday. "This time, they'll let me try."

But when they got to the park, it was the same old story.

Mina begged to have a go on the bike.

And her mum and dad listed all the reasons why this was a very bad idea.

"You're just too small!" said Mum.

"You're just not strong enough!" said Dad.

"But I am strong!" cried Mina. "Look!"

And she did 50 sit-ups …

and 100 star jumps …

and picked up Ayman's bike to show them her muscles.

"Oh, be careful!" wailed Mum.

"Don't hurt yourself!" shouted Dad. "Put it down!"

Mina put the bike down.

"Maybe next week," said Mum.

Mina knew that next week would never come. But she wasn't going to give up. She was just going to have to think of a different plan. A big one.

And think of one she did.

In the summer holidays,
Mum and Dad had to carry on working,
so Grandpa Harry would come to stay
to look after Mina May and Ayman.

Grandpa Harry was a lot less worried
about Mina May than Mum and Dad.

"Can I climb the tree?" Mina May
would ask.

"Of course, you can!" Grandpa Harry
would reply. "The higher the better!"

"Can I roller skate down the garden path?" Mina May would ask.

"Of course, you can!" Grandpa Harry would reply. "The faster the better!"

And even though she was allowed to go high and fast, Mina May was always very sensible.

"What have you two been up to today?" Mum would ask when she got in.

"Not much," Mina May would say.

"The usual," Ayman would add.

Grandpa Harry was Mina May's big plan. And he was coming tomorrow morning.

"So, what larks do you two want to get up to today?" asked Grandpa Harry, as soon as Mum and Dad had shut the front door.

"We could tunnel under the house!" suggested Ayman, who was very fond of tunnelling.

"Interesting," said Grandpa Harry. "But a bit messy. Anything else?"

"We could have a bonfire!" suggested Ayman, who was very fond of fires as well.

"Interesting," said Grandpa Harry. "But a bit hot. Anything else?"

"I've got an idea," said Mina. "And it's not messy or hot."

"Go on," said Grandpa.

"OK." Mina took a big breath for her big moment. "You could teach me to ride a bike."

Grandpa Harry smiled. "That sounds like just the ticket," he said. "What do you reckon, Ayman?"

"A million per cent!" said Ayman, who was fond of exaggerating too.

"First, we need some equipment," said Mina May, who had read a lot about bikes while she was sitting on the bench.

In the attic, they found Ayman's old helmet, elbow pads and kneepads. And, because Mina May was so small, they fitted her perfectly.

"Next, we need a bike," said Ayman, who was eager to help some more.

14

In the garage, they found Ayman's old bike. And, because Mina May was so small, she could sit on it easily.

"Now we need somewhere to ride!" said Grandpa.

"Somewhere fast!" said Ayman. "With bumps and jumps and massive hills!"

"Somewhere safe!" said Mina, who was still very sensible, despite her excitement. "With grass for a soft landing in case I come off."

The park was the perfect place.

"Ready?" asked Grandpa Harry, as Mina May sat in the saddle and looked at the long stretch of green ahead.

"As I'll ever be," she replied.

"Then we're off!"

At first, Grandpa Harry held on to the back of the bike, so Mina May could get used to pedalling.

Up and down, they trundled, again and again, Mina May's legs pumping, Grandpa panting, and Ayman cycling beside them.

"Go on, Mina May!" her brother whooped. "You can do it!"

"Amazing," said Grandpa. "You were born to ride!"

But, even though she felt like she was flying, Mina May knew Grandpa was still holding on tightly.

"You can let go soon!" she yelled. "I think I've got it!"

"What do you mean?" came Grandpa Harry's voice from far behind her. "I let go long ago!"

As soon as she realised that, Mina May began
to wibble ...

and wobble ...

"Steady!" called Grandpa Harry.

"Look straight ahead!" cried Ayman.

And Mina May did. She steadied herself and looked in
front of her, and soon the bike was gliding again, without
a single wibble or the slightest wobble.

"I'm doing it!" she yelled. "I'm really doing it!"

And she was. Even though she was not much taller than a tall dog, and not quite as strong as an ox, Mina May Malek was cycling all by herself.

She went across the grass …

around the path …

and all the way back to the house.

"What have you two been up to today?" asked Mum, when she got in.

"Not much," said Mina May.

"The usual," added Ayman.

"Don't look at me," said Grandpa Harry, with a wink to Mina.

Every day, Mina May, Ayman and Grandpa Harry went to the park. And every day, Ayman and all Ayman's friends taught Mina May how to do tricks.

One day, when she was learning to rock walk, she spun too hard and found herself flung into the air.

Then she landed with a thud on the mud.

"Oh no!" yelled Leon.

"Wait there!" called Connor.

"Oops-a-daisy," said Grandpa Harry.

Mina tried to hide her tears. She wasn't badly hurt, but she was worried what her parents might say.

"But look," said Ayman. "The elbow pads and kneepads have protected you!"

"You can't tell a thing," agreed Leon.

"Falling off is all part of the fun," said Grandpa Harry. "You've just got to get back in the saddle."

And, wiping her eyes, Mina did.

Soon, Mina got so good, she could outshine even Ayman. But she was still a little sad: her mum and dad had no idea how extraordinary their daughter was.

Until one morning, she and Ayman and Grandpa Harry saw a sign in the park.

"Kids' Bike Competition this Saturday," it read. *"Show us your stunts!"*

"What do you think?" asked Grandpa Harry. "Game for it, Ayman?"

"Definitely," said Ayman. "I'll sign up as soon as we get home!"

"What about you?" Grandpa looked at Mina May.

"I – " Mina thought for a moment. This was it! This was her chance to show her parents what she was made of. But what if they found out before and tried to stop her? Unless … "I suppose I could," she continued. "But with one little difference – "

"Well, I can't wait to watch," said Dad, as he helped Ayman find his things for the competition.

"Don't forget his helmet," added Mum.

"And his kneepads," said Mina May, handing them over helpfully.

"You can always come too," said Mum.

"I'll be OK with Grandpa," Mina May replied.

"I wonder who this 'Marvellous M' is," pondered Dad, reading the leaflet. "One to watch, eh, Ayman?"

"For sure." Ayman nodded, and winked at Mina May. "See you later!"

Mina May winked back. "You will!"

No sooner was the front door closed than Mina May and Grandpa scooted out of the back where her bike, helmet and pads were waiting.

"Ready?" Grandpa Harry asked.

Mina May grinned. "As I'll ever be," she said.

And off they set to the park.

Ayman was up first.

Mina May felt her heart pitter-patter, as her brother alley-ooped, bunny hopped and rock walked like a pro, only making two tiny mistakes.

"Your go," said Grandpa.

Mina May eyed the crowd where her mum and dad were cheering her brother on. "It's now or never," she said, bike teetering at the top of the ramp.

She took a big breath, and then let her bike slide forwards.

Now she really was flying, down and up and down the ramp again, barspinning and backflipping and showing everyone what Marvellous M was made of.

As she came to a halt, the crowd went wild.

It's time, she thought. And setting her bike on the ground, she whipped off her helmet and mask, and stared straight at Mum and Dad.

"What?" cried Mum.

"Who?" wailed Dad.

"How?" demanded Mum.

"Why?" added Dad.

Mina smiled. "Because I can," she said. "I may be small, but I'm strong."

Then a wonderful thing happened. Dad smiled. "Mina May Malek," he said. "You're as strong as an ox."

"Stronger than Ayman," said Mum, hardly believing it, but smiling too.

"Maybe somewhere in the middle," laughed Grandpa Harry. "She's a champion, in any case."

And she was. Marvellous Mina beat off all the competition to take home first prize.

From that day on, Mina May was allowed to do everything that Ayman did …

climbing trees …

roller skating …

canoeing …

jumping off a diving board …

and eating strawberries.

But they still haven't tunnelled next door or made a bonfire … yet …

Mina's diary

5th March

I had to sit on the bench again today. It's not fair. Why does Ayman get to do everything, and I can't do anything at all? I haven't been ill in AGES and I never have accidents. He's always the one getting bruises at football, and Mum just says, "Never mind, Ayman," or, "You're all right, aren't you, Ayman?"

Sometimes I wish I was Ayman.

Mum's diary

5th March

   Poor Mina. I know it must be hard for her having to watch Ayman instead of joining in. But she can't remember how scary it was when she was small and ill. And how fragile her bones were for so long. I know the doctors say she's fine now, but I'm her mum so, of course, I worry.

   I wish I could help her understand.

 Ideas for reading

Written by Gill Matthews
Primary Literacy Consultant

Reading objectives:
- ask questions to improve understanding of a text
- draw inferences such as inferring characters' feelings, thoughts and motives from their actions and justifying inferences with evidence
- predict what might happen from details stated and implied
- identify how language, structure and presentation contribute to meaning

Spoken language objectives:
- ask relevant questions to extend their understanding and knowledge
- articulate and justify answers, arguments and opinions
- use spoken language to develop understanding through speculating, hypothesising, imagining and exploring ideas

Curriculum links: Relationships education – Families and people who care for me; Caring friendships

Interest words: cried, pleaded, begged, worried

Build a context for reading
- Ask children to look at the front cover and read the title. Ask them to explain what they think the word *marvellous* means.
- Read the back-cover blurb. Discuss why Mina might be marvellous. Ask children what they think *they* are marvellous at doing.
- Ask children why they think Mina's parents won't let her become a BMX champ. Ask if there is anything *their* parents won't let them do.

Understand and apply reading strategies
- Read pp2–5 aloud to the children. Ask what kind of person they think Mina is. Discuss whether they think it is fair that her parents don't let her do things, considering both Mina's point of view and those of her parents.
- Encourage children to predict what Mina is going to do next and how she might make herself *as strong as an ox*.